Book 1
Facebook Social Power
BY SAM KEY

&

Book 2
Windows 8 Tips for Beginners
BY SAM KEY

Book 1
Facebook Social Power

BY SAM KEY

The Most Powerful Represented Facebook Guide to Making Money on anything on the Planet!

Programming Box Set #84: Facebook Social Power & Windows 8 Tips for Beginners

Programming Box Set #84: Facebook Social Power & Windows 8 Tips for Beginners

Table Of Contents

Introduction

I want to thank you and congratulate you for purchasing the book, "Learning the Social Power of Facebook: The Most Powerful Represented Facebook Guide to Making Money on anything on the Planet!"

This book contains proven steps and strategies on how to learn ways to use Facebook as a means to generate money for whatever business you have.

As you well may know by now, Facebook can be an amazing tool to promote your business, and of course, make money from it. However, not everyone knows how to do it, but with the help of this book, you'll learn everything you need to know about how to use Facebook to attract people's attention, and be successful in the world of business.

What are you waiting for? Start reading this book now and make money through Facebook as soon as possible!

Thanks again for purchasing this book, I hope you enjoy it!

Chapter 1: Make Use of Advertising based on E-Commerce

Because of Facebook's Ad Platform, a lot of marketers have been able to reach a wide range of audience because they get to put ads on their Facebook Pages that takes those who click the links to E-Commerce sites, so just the fact that these people get to see their pages already add a lot of traffic to their sites, and may allow people to get paid.

Oftentimes, people overlook the ads-to-direct sites but knowing how to go forth with it is very beneficial because it has a three-way approach that will help you earn a lot of money. Basically, this approach goes as follows:

FB Ads—Discount Pages/Website Sales—Buyers/Customers

One example of a company that benefited a lot from E-Commerce based Advertising through Facebook is Vamplets.com. Vamplets.com is popular for selling plush dolls—but these dolls aren't just regular plush dolls, as they are Vampire Plushies. When Vamplets used this kind of advertising, they were able to achieve 300% ROI, which is definitely a mean feat.

So, how then are you going to be able to use E-Commerce based Advertising for your business? Follow the pointers below and you'll understand how.

Choose your Audience

First and foremost, you have to choose your target demographic so that sales funnel will be easier to be filled. Facebook will allow you to choose between one of the following:

- Custom Audience from Your Website
- Custom Audience from MailChimp
- Data File Custom Audience
- Custom Audience from Your Mobile App

Once you're able to choose your target demographic, it will be easy for you to convert an ad to money because these people will be interested in what you have to offer because you're no longer going to be generalizing things.

You can also choose your audience via the Facebook Audience Insights Category. Here, you'll be able to find people who are interested in your campaign, based on pages that they have liked, so that you'd know that they would like to see what your business is all about. This is called interest-based campaigning.

You can also try using Lookalike Audiences. You can do this by making use of your existing audience, and then pick the next group of people who act and feel similar to your original audience so your posts would be able to reach more people, and you'd get more traffic and revenue, as well. It would be nice to test audiences, too, so you'd know who's interested in your services.

For example, you're selling clothes for pregnant women. You really cannot expect people who are single or who are still in High School click your ads, or like your page, because of course, they're not in that stage of their lives yet. So, make sure that you choose audiences that you know will listen to what you have to say.

Then, go on and place a Facebook Pixel to the footer of your page, and your ads will then be connected to Facebook. You can also choose to send traffic to one audience group this week, then to another group the next.

Make Proper Segments for Visitors of Your Homepage

Of course, you have to make sure that your homepage gets the attention of many because if it doesn't, and if people feel alienated by it, you also cannot expect that you'll gain profit from it. The three basic things that you have to have in your homepage include:

- New Sales Items
- Branding Ads
- Other Promotional Ads

Make Segments for Categories and Products

You can also place ads in various categories of your website so that even if your customer does not check out all the items he placed in the cart, your website will still gain some revenue because more often than not, customers like to buy products based on ads that were able to get through to them.

Chapter 2: Use Fan Marketing E-Commerce

Basically, Fan Marketing E-Commerce is the means of promoting your business by making sure that you post ads through your page and have those ads appear on the newsfeeds of your target demographic.

Research has it that fans become more interested in a new product or business when they see ads, instead of when they learn about the said products through contests or just from other people. Why? Simply because ads are more professional ways of getting people's attention and marketing products, and Facebook definitely makes that easy.

However, it's not enough that you just have a fanpage. You have to make sure that you actually use the said page and that it doesn't get stuck. You can do this by making sure that you constantly post a thing or two, and that you interact with your fans, as well.

You see, a study held in 2011 showed that although over a hundred thousand people may like a certain page, sometimes, revenue only gets up by 7%, because the owners of the fan pages do not interact with their fans and have not posted anything in a while. You also have to make sure that you stay relevant by being able to attract new fans from time to time.

Once you do this right, you'll be able to create the process of:

FB Ads—FB Fans—See Posts—Click to Website—Buyers/Customers

Some of those who have greatly benefited from Fan Marketing Strategies include:

- Baseball Roses, a company that sells artificial roses made from old baseball balls, who gained over 437% of ROI with the help of Facebook Fan Marketing;
- Superherostuff.com, a website that sells merchandise based on famous superheroes, such as t-shirts, jackets, hoodies, shoes, and more, gained over 150% ROI, and;

- Rosehall Kennel Breeds, a company that specializes in selling German Shepherds, gained over a whopping 4,000% of ROI for its fan acquisition speed alone—and that's definitely something that should inspire you.

So, what exactly did these companies do and how did they make use of Facebook Fan Marketing E-Commerce for their own benefit? Here are some tips that you can follow:

1. **Make sure that you post a new update after your last update is gone from people's newsfeeds.** Sometimes, you see posts in your feed for even a day or two after posting, but there are also times when they are gone after just a couple of minutes or hours. It actually varies due to how fans see or react on those posts and Facebook's EdgeRank Algorithm will be able to give you a glimpse of how your post is doing, based on three main factors, which are:

    a. **Likes per Post.** You'd know that people are interested in your posts when they actually make it a point to like the said posts, and it's great because likes are always updated in real time, and will also let your posts stay longer on people's newsfeeds. Therefore, make sure to check the numbers of likes regularly.

    b. **Comments per Post.** Comments are always time-stamped, but you cannot always rely on these as not everyone like to comment on posts, and you cannot define whether the posts appear on people's feeds, or they're simply too lazy to comment.

    c. **Impressions per Post.** This is basically the number of times a single status has been viewed. While the numbers update as more and more people get to see your post, there are also times when the number stay stagnant only because Facebook refuses to update, so may have to wait a while to see the real numbers.

A good way of trying to gauge your influence on Facebook is by posting an hourly status, then make sure that you record the number of likes, comments, and impressions, and then record the data on Excel. Make a graph, then see the ratio of how much your posts appear on one's feeds, and decide the average number of posts that you have to do per day or per week.

2. **Make sure that the things you post are not redundant.** People these days have really short attention span so it would be nice if you know how to post varied content. Make sure that your fans have something to come back to each day, and that they don't get bored with whatever it is that you have on your website and won't click the "dislike" button.
3. **Do some marketing.** Again, you're trying to make money by means of promoting your products so you have to do a lot of marketing via Facebook. An easy way of doing this is by giving your fans discount codes that they can use if they're interested in buying your products so that they'd constantly check your page.
4. **Make sure that social sharing buttons are open.** While you may use Facebook as the original platform for advertising your services, you also have to realize that it's important to share your content on other websites or social networking sites so that more people would get to see what you have to offer. Also, make sure that your page is set to public because you really cannot expect people to know what you want them to know if your page is set to private. When your page is public, they'll be able to like, comment, and share your posts, which will bring you more traffic and more revenue. Then, connect your Facebook Page to your other social media accounts so that whenever you post updates on your Facebook Page, the updates will be sent to all your other accounts, as well.
5. **Don't ever try hard-selling tactics.** It's always better to be subtle because people hate it when they feel like their feeds are full of pages that just sell their products outright without making the fans understand what they're all about. So, try asking your fans some questions, or create polls about what kind of products or services they like but never just put up ads or ask them to "buy your products" right away without helping them know that you're their "friend" and that you want them to know what's best in the market right now. You can also place behind the scenes videos of what goes on in your company, or

post testimonials from past customers to get the curiosity of your fans running. This way, you get to be trustworthy and your business will be more authoritative, and people would be more interested.

6. **And, make sure that you provide good customer service.** For a Facebook Page to be successful, it doesn't have to be bombarded with ads, you also have to make sure that you get to be friends with your customers and that loyalty and trust are built. For example, when one of your fans posts questions or queries on your page, take time to answer the said questions, and make sure that you reply as soon as possible so that you get to create some sense of urgency and that people will know that you're there.

Keep these tips in mind and you'll surely be able to make use of your Facebook Page to give you a lot of profit. Oh, and make sure to have ample amounts of patience, too!

Chapter 3: Connect Facebook Ads to E-Mail

Another way of making use of Facebook to gain revenue is by connecting ads to e-mails. Basically, it's a way of promoting content to your e-mail subscribers so that it will be easier for your fans to know about your new products or services, or to know if there are contests or events coming up based on the updates that you have sent.

Basically, when Facebook ads are sent to people's e-mails, there are more chances of acquiring a larger number of future subscribers. And Facebook makes this easy for you as they have a feature that allows you to add E-mail lists to your Fan Page so that whenever you post an update, your e-mail list will automatically get to know it, too.

The target formula is as follows:

FB Ad—Squeeze—E-mail Sign Up—E-mail Open—E-mail Click to Visit—Buyers/Customers

So, in order for you to be successful in this kind of marketing tactic, you first have to get a target demographic of e-mail subscribers. While it may be easy to just post an invite so your fans would want to be part of your e-mail list, it will be nice to filter people who probably won't open your e-mails and choose people who would be interested in what you have to offer. You can do this by adding information to the Facebook Ad Copy Page. The information that you need are as follows:

- Gender
- Age
- Location
- Interests
- Relationship Status
- Educational Attainment/Level
- Workplace
- Pages that have been liked (So you'd get to see if they would like the posts that you'd be making)

Then, go on and upload the e-mail list on your Facebook Page by giving Facebook a list of e-mails from MailChimp or any other AutoResponder Service, so that the e-mail addresses of your fans will be synchronized to your page.

Effective Message Integration

It's so easy to send a message but it's never really easy to make sure that those messages are effective. However, there are a couple of tips that you can keep in mind:

- Optimize Facebook Ad Headlines with Catchy Subject Lines so that your fans will be interested to open your e-mails. Examples include:
    - Do Gamers dream of DOTA II?
    - Why your 12 year old likes Miley Cyrus
    - 8 Most Annoying Social Media Moments of 2014
    - 3 Ways to Improve Your Life

  Basically, you have to make sure that your subject lines have a lot to do with your content and with your line of business so that your fans won't be confused and they'd be interested in what you have to say.
- Add your fans' testimonials and comments about your services so others would know that you are for real.
- Add images into your e-mails. After all, people have short attention span and they would appreciate it if they get to see images as part of your e-mails because these would get their attention more and would help them picture what you are talking about.
- Let your fans know that you are going to send another e-mail blast by updating your Facebook status.
- Tease some of the contents of your e-mail on your status updates so that your fans will be hyped up and will be curious to open their e-mails.

- Make use of Facebook Landing Tabs, and Social Log-in Software, so that whenever your fans open their e-mails, it will automatically add traffic to your Facebook Page, and your website, as well.
- Put some sort of disclaimer, or a line that allows your fans to unsubscribe if they want to, because they have to know that you're not actually forcing them to read your messages and that they have the choice to unsubscribe from your list.
- And don't forget to send Thank You messages. If you want to foster a great relationship with your fans, you have to let them know that you're thankful that they're around, and that they're part of your list, so that they will realize that it's substantial to read the content that you are sending, and that it's important to be a fan of yours, instead of just talking about yourself all the time, without thinking of your fans. After all, without them, you won't gain any profit so you have to be grateful that they're around.

You can also run Geo-targeted ads, or ads that are meant for people who live in one location alone, so that the e-mails would feel more personal and so that your fans will know that you are really thinking of them. Sometimes, targeting people who are in the same vicinity as you is more effective because you get to really connect with them as you experience the same things and you'd know that they are more likely to try your products, unlike those that live in far away places.

If you're able to be successful with Facebook E-mail marketing, you can definitely gain more traffic and more revenue. One of those Fortune 500 Companies actually gained 400% ROI just because of its e-mail subscribers, so you can expect that you'll gain more, too, but only if you follow the tips given above. Good Luck!

Chapter 4: Making Use of Your Ad-Supported Sites

Ad-Supported sites are those that run advertisements and allow the said ads to be shared to your Facebook Page.

This is especially helpful for those whose businesses are really situated online, and those whose blogs or websites are their bread and butter. So, if that's the case, it would be important to create a Facebook Page that's connected to your blog or your website so that things would be formalized more. People like it when they see that a certain website has a Facebook Page because they feel like they'd get to be updated more without having to go to the website.

The formula for this is as follows:

FB Ad—FB Fan—See Post—Click to Website—Click Ad

So basically, when people click ads on your website that take them to your Facebook Page and Vice Versa, you not only gain traffic, you get to be paid, as well. This is similar as the popular Pay-Per-Click Advertising tactic. And also, when you get more fans from various parts of the world, your revenue will increase even more mainly because your content now gets to reach a large number of people, which evidently is beneficial for your business.

Proud Single Moms, a site targeted to help single mothers, gained over $5,000 for Facebook Ads alone that were promoted on their Facebook Page that has around 100,000 fans. On their blog, they made sure that they posted topics that single mothers would be able to relate to, and they also made sure that they used keywords that would give them high search rank on search engines such as Google, or Yahoo.

You can make use of Keyword Tools that are found online to find the perfect keywords that are related to your niche. Once you use these keywords in your posts, you'll be able to generate traffic and revenue.

The main reason why ads on Facebook are so effective is the fact that almost everyone in the world has a Facebook account, so of course, you can expect them to see your posts and the ads that are on your page, too. Plus, when you post links of your blog's content to your Facebook Page, there are more chances that people will get to read these posts because of course, they found it on Facebook, and they didn't use the web just so they could see your website. And these days, that is very important. The key is to be reachable.

Proud Single Moms made sure that they posted the links of blog post updates each day and in just a matter of six months, they were able to create another website that gave them more revenue.

Chapter 5: Other Tips

Aside from the techniques given above, you can also make use of these Facebook Marketing tactics to make sure that your business gains more profit:

Ads through SMS

While it may not be as popular as other Facebook Marketing tips, the combination of Facebook Ads and Text Messaging have slowly been gaining the attention of many for being a fast-paced approach when it comes to advertising products and services. In fact, around 24% of marketers on mobile have gained more ROI just because people have responded to text messages regarding product promotions, and have tried the coupons that they gave away through text, too.

This is especially effective for those with business that are related to food as free coupons that were sent to Facebook fans helped these fans to be more interested to try certain products that were being sold, and have visited the restaurants more often in hopes that they'd be given more information and more freebies, too. When people feel like they know the latest news about a certain establishment or a certain product, it's easy for them to appreciate the said establishment and so they get to patronize it more. This then gave the restaurants around $60,000 more revenue, which is definitely something good!

Give Some Offers that they won't be able to refuse!

Mostly everyone want freebies, because money is really hard to come by these days and not everything is affordable, so of course, they feel like it's nice to be able to get some goodies or services for free. Facebook Offers actually help you create deals with your fans that are not available on other social media platforms.

Basically, you ask your customers to like your page and leave their e-mail addresses so that you can send them coupons or offers that they can redeem in your store. First, make the offers exclusive to your fans then when it gets successful, you can then make more offers for people outside your circle so that more people would be excited to try your products and see what you have to offer.

Don't think about losing profit. More often than not, when you give things away for free, people will be more interested to try your other products and so of course, they'd be paying you in the future, so it's like you have made them your investment and soon enough, you'll benefit from them.

Create Apps for them

A lot of people these days rely on apps that they could use to open certain websites or pages, and of course, if you create an app for your business, it will be easy for them to read your content and it will be easy for you to reach them. They wouldn't have to deal with the hassle of using the browser just so they could see some offers or read articles connected to a certain topic that they would like to learn about. Also, it's better if you add links to your Facebook Page to the app that you have created so that everything will be merged together.

You can also create Facebook Ads without creating a Facebook Page

You can do this by selecting the Clicks to Website option of Facebook or the Website Conversions tab. People will still get to see your ads on the right side of their pages. You know, those ads that appear near the chat sidebar, so in a way, you still get to promote your business, but having Facebook Pages are still way better because then the ads appear on the main feeds and not just on the right side tabs.

Create a catchy headline

Just like how important it is to create effective e-mail subject lines, it's also important to create catchy ad headlines because these will attract people's attention and will allow people to understand what you and your business are all about.

The rule of thumb is to make sure that the headline of your ad is the same as the title of your page so it will be easily recognizable. It would also be helpful if you pair it up with an image that you have created so that people will be able to connect the said image to your business and it will be easy for them to remember your ad.

Make use of Sponsored Stories, too

You see, sponsored stories are the results of how people interact on your page or how they appreciate your content. Basically, whenever someone likes your posts or updates, or when they comment on or share your content, it creates “Facebook Stories”. To make sure that these stories appear on a lot of people’s newsfeeds, you have to pay a minimal fee, so it’s like you get to easily advertise your content and you make sure that people actually get to see them.

But make sure that you choose the best bidding and advertising options

What’s good about Facebook is that it allows you to choose the best kind of bidding option that will be good for your business. For example, you can choose whether you want to gain revenue through clicks, or through impressions then you can then reach your objective after you have customized your bids.

You can also choose whether you’d like to pay for your content to be advertised by paying daily, or by paying for a lifetime. The advantages of paying for a lifetime is that you’d know that your content will always be published and that you’d basically have nothing else to worry about, but the thing is that when you want to change the products you are advertising or if you’re going to close your business down, it’s like you’ll get people confused because they’ll still see ads from your old site, and they’d keep looking for your services. So, it’s recommended that you just pay for the ads daily or on a case to case basis, say there’s an event that’s coming up and the like, so that it won’t be hard for you to reach your followers and gain potential fans in the process, too.

When making use of image ads, make sure that text is only 20%

You would not want to bombard your followers with too many texts and images in just one post. Plus, your image ads won’t be approved if they contain more than 20% of text.

In order to know if your ads are following Facebook’s guidelines, check out the Facebook Grid Tool that will help you see how your ad looks and what needs to be changed, if necessary.

Let others help you

Sometimes, two heads are better than one, and it's great because when you add another admin to your page, they can also update your page so whenever you're busy or if you cannot answer queries right away, these other admins can help you out.

Just make sure that you choose admins that you can trust and that they know a lot about your business so the things they will be posting will be substantial, too. To do this, just go to the Ad Manager option of Facebook, then click Ad Account Roles, and choose Add a User. Make sure that the person you will add as an admin is your friend on Facebook and that his e-mail address can easily be searched through Facebook, too.

And, don't forget to choose the revenue model that is right for you

To do this, you may have to try each technique first, but don't worry because sooner or later, you'll find the one that proves to be the most effective for your business.

In the marketing business, trial and error really is one of the biggest keys to success, so don't worry if you feel like you aren't being successful right away. Take chances and soon enough, you'll be on the path to success. Good Luck!

Conclusion

Thank you again for purchasing this book!

I hope this book was able to help you understand how you can use Facebook to advertise your business and gain lots of revenue.

The next step is to follow the techniques listed here, and don't be afraid to try each one because sooner or later, you'll find the perfect fit for you. Advertise through Facebook and let your business soar!

Thank you and good luck!

Book 2
Windows 8 Tips for Beginners

BY SAM KEY

A Simple, Easy, and Efficient Guide to a Complex System of Windows 8!

Programming Box Set #84: Facebook Social Power & Windows 8 Tips for Beginners

Table Of Contents

Introduction

I want to thank you and congratulate you for purchasing the book, "Windows 8 Tips for Beginners: A Simple, easy, and efficient guide to a complex system of windows 8!"

This book contains proven steps and strategies on how to familiarize yourself with the new features of Windows 8 which were designed to make your computing experience simpler and more enjoyable. You will not only learn how to navigate through Windows 8 , but you will also learn how Windows 8 is similar to and different from the older versions so you can easily adjust and take advantage of the benefits that Windows 8 has in store for you.

Thanks again for purchasing this book, I hope you enjoy it!

Chapter 1: How is Windows 8 Different from Previous Versions?

With Windows 8, Microsoft launched a lot of new changes and features, some of which are minor , but others are major. Some of the changes you can see in Windows 8 are the redesigned interface, enhanced security and other online features.

Changes in the Interface

The most glaring change you will observe when you first open your computer with Windows 8 is that the screen looks completely different from older Windows versions. The Windows 8 interface has new features such as Start screen, hot corners, and live tiles.

- The Start screen will be the main screen where you will find all of your installed programs and they will be in the form of "tiles". You can personalize your Start Screen by rearranging the tiles, selecting a background image and changing the color scheme.

- You can navigate through Windows 8 using the "hot corners", which you activate by hovering the mouse pointer over the corners of the screen. For instance, if you want to switch to another open application, hover your mouse in the top-left corner of your screen and then click on the app.

- Certain apps have Live Tile functions, which enable you to see information even if the app itself is not open. For instance, you can easily see the current weather on the Weather app tile from your Start screen; if you want to see more information, you can just click on the app to open it.

- You can now find many of the settings of your computer in the Charms bar that you can open by hovering the mouse in the bottom-right or top-right corner of your computer screen.

Online Features in Windows 8

Because of the ease of accessing Internet now, many people have started to save their documents and other data online. Microsoft has made it easier to save on the cloud through their OneDrive service (this was formerly called SkyDrive). Windows 8 is capable of linking to OneDrive and other online social networks such as Twitter and Facebook in a seamless manner.

To connect your computer to OneDrive, sign in using your free Microsoft account instead of your own computer account. When you do this, all of the contacts, files and other information stored in your OneDrive are all in your Start screen. You can also use another computer to sign in to your Microsoft account and access all of your OneDrive files. You can also easily link your Flickr, Twitter and Facebook accounts to Windows 8 so you will be able to see the updates straight from your Start screen. You can also do this through the People app which is included in Windows 8.

Other Features

- The Desktop is now simpler for enhanced speed. Yes, the Desktop is still included in Windows 8 and you can still manage your documents or open your installed programs through the Desktop. However, with Windows 8, a number of the transparency effects that frequently caused Windows Vista and Windows 7 to slow down are now gone. This allows the Desktop to operate smoother on nearly all computers.

- The Start menu, once considered as a vital feature in previous Windows versions, is now the Start screen. You can now open your installed programs or search for your files through the Start screen. This can be quite disorienting if you are just starting with Windows 8.

- Windows 8 has enhanced security because of its integrated antivirus program referred to as Windows Defender. This antivirus program is also useful in protecting you from different kinds of malware. In addition, it can aid in keeping you and your computer secure by telling you which data each of your installed apps can access. For instance, certain apps can access your location, so if you do not want other people to know where you are, just change your preference in the settings/configuration part of your apps.

How to Use Windows 8

Because Windows 8 is not like the older versions, it will possibly change how you have been using your computer. You may need quite some time to get accustomed to the new features, but you just need to remember that those changes are necessary to enhance your computing experience. For instance, if you have used older Windows versions, you may be used to clicking on the Start button to launch programs. You need to get used to using the Start screen with Windows 8. Of course, you can still use the Desktop view to make file and folder organization easier and to launch older programs.

You may need to switch between the Desktop view and the Start screen to work on your computer. Don't feel bad if you feel disoriented at first because you will get used to it. Moreover, if you just use your computer to surf the internet, you may be spending majority of your time in the Start screen anyway.

Chapter 2: How to Get Started with Windows 8

Windows 8 can truly be bewildering at the start because of the many changes done to the interface. You will need to learn effective navigation of both the Start screen and Desktop view. Even though the Desktop view appears similar to the older Windows versions, it has one major change that you need to get used to – the Start menu is no more.

In this chapter, you will learn how to work with the apps and effectively navigate Windows 8 using the Charms bar. You will learn where to look for the features that you could previously find in the Start menu.

How to Sign In

While setting up Windows 8, you will be required to create your own account name and password that you will use to sign in. You can also opt to create other account names and associate each account name with a specific Microsoft account. You will then see your own user account name and photo (if you have uploaded one). Key in your password and press enter. To select another user, click on the back arrow to choose from the available options. After you have signed in, the Start screen will be displayed.

How to Navigate Windows 8

You can use the following ways to navigate your way through Windows 8

- You can use the hot corners to navigate through Windows 8. You can use them whether you are in the Desktop view or in the Start screen. Simply hover your mouse in the corner of the screen to access the hot corners. You will see a tile or a toolbar that you can then click to open. All the corners perform various tasks. For instance, hovering the pointer on the lower-left corner will return you to the Start screen. The upper-left corner will allow you to switch to the last application that you were using. The lower-right or upper-right corners gives you access to the Charms bar where you can either manage your printers or adjust the settings of your computer. Hover your mouse towards the upper-left corner and then move your mouse down to see the list of the different applications that you are simultaneously using. You can simply on any application to go back to it.

- You can also navigate through Windows 8 through different keyboard shortcuts.
  - Alt+Tab is the most useful shortcut; you use it to switch between open applications in both the Start screen and Desktop view.
  - You can use the Windows key to go back to the Start screen. It also works in both the Desktop view and Start screen.
  - From the Start screen, you can go to the Desktop view by clicking on Windows+D.
- You can access the settings and other features of your computer through the toolbar referred to as Charms bar. Place your mouse pointer on the bottom-right or top-right corner of your screen to display the Charms bar wherein you can see the following icons or "charms":
  - The Search charm allows you to look for files, apps or settings on your computer. However, a simpler method to do a search is through the Start screen wherein you can simply key in the name of the application or file that you want to find.
  - You can think of the Share charm as a "copy and paste" attribute that is included in Windows 8 to make it easier for you to work with your computer. Using the Share charm, you can "copy" data like a web address or a picture from one app and then "paste" it onto another application. For instance, if you are reading a certain article in the Internet, you can share the website address in your Mail application so you can send it to a friend.
  - The Start charm will allow you to go back to the Start screen. If you are currently on the Start screen, the Start charm will launch the latest app that you used.

- The Devices charm displays all of the hardware devices that are linked to your computer such as monitors and printers.
- Through the Settings charm, you can open both the general setting of your computer and the settings of the application that you are presently using. For instance, if you are presently using the web browser, you can access the Internet Options through the Settings charm.

How to Work with the Start Screen Applications

You may need to familiarize yourself with the Start screen applications because they are quite different from the "classic" Windows applications from previous versions. The apps in Windows 8 fill the whole screen rather than launching in a window. However, you can still do multi-tasking by launching two or more applications next to each other.

- To open an application from the Start screen, look for the app that you want to launch and click on it.
- To close an application hover your mouse at the top portion of the application, and you will notice that the cursor will become a hand icon, click and hold your mouse and then drag it towards the bottommost part of the screen and then release. When the app has closed, you will go back to the Start screen.

How to View Apps Side by Side

Even though the applications normally fill up the whole screen, Windows 8 still allows you to snap an application to the right or left side and then launch other applications beside it. For instance, you can work on a word document while viewing the calendar app. Here are the steps to view applications side by side:

1. Go to the Start screen and then click on the first app that you want to open.
2. Once the app is open, click on the title bar and drag the window to the left or right side of your computer screen.

3. Release your mouse and you will see that the application has snapped to the side of your computer screen.

4. You can go back to the Start screen by clicking at any empty space of the computer screen.

5. Click on another application that you want to open.

6. You will now see the applications displayed side by side. You can also adjust the size of the applications by dragging the bar.

Please note that the snapping feature is intended to work with a widescreen monitor. Your minimum screen resolution should be 1366 x 768 pixels to enjoy the snapping feature fully. If your monitor has a bigger screen, you will be able to snap more than two apps simultaneously.

How to cope with the Start menu

Many people have already complained about the missing Start menu in Windows 8. For many Windows users, the Start menu is a very vital feature because they use to open applications, look for files, launch the Control Panel and shut down their computer. You can actually do all of these things in Windows 8 too, but you will now have to look for them in different locations.

- There are a number of ways to launch an application in Windows 8. You can launch an app by clicking the application icon on the taskbar or double-clicking the application shortcut form the Desktop view or clicking the application tile in the Start screen.

- You can look for an app or a file by pressing the Windows key to go back to the Start screen. When you are there, you can simply key in the filename or app name that you want to look for. The results of your search will be immediately displayed underneath the search bar. You will also see a list of recommended web searches underneath the search results.

- You can launch the Control Panel by going to the Desktop view and then hovering your mouse in the lower-right corner of the computer screen to display the Charms bar and then selecting Settings. From the Settings Pane, look for and choose Control Panel.

After the Control Panel pops up, you can start choosing your preferred settings.

- You can shut down your computer by hovering the mouse in the lower-right corner of your screen to display the Charms bar and then selecting Settings. Click on the Power icon and then choose Shut Down.

Start Screen Options

If you prefer to continue working with the Desktop view more often, you actually have a number of alternatives that can let your computer operate more like the older Windows versions. One of these alternatives is the "boot your computer directly to the Desktop" rather than the Start screen. Here are the steps to change your Start screen options:

1. Return to the Desktop view.
2. Right-click the taskbar then choose Properties.
3. You will then see a dialog box where you can choose the options that you want to change.

Chapter 3: How to Personalize Your Start Screen

If you are open to the idea of spending most of your time on the Start screen of your computer, there are different ways you can do to personalize it based on your preferences. You can change the background color and image, rearrange the applications, pin applications and create application groups.

- You can change the background of your Start screen by hovering the mouse in the lower-right corner of your screen to open up the Charms bar and then selecting the Settings icon. Choose Personalize and then choose your preferred color scheme and background image.

- You can change the lock screen picture by displaying the Charms bar again and the selecting the Settings icon. Choose Change PC settings and then choose Lock screen that is located near to the topmost part of the screen. Choose your preferred image from the thumbnail photos shown. You can also opt to click on Browse to choose your own photos. You will see the lock screen every time you return to your computer after leaving it inactive for a set number of minutes. However, you can also manually lock your screen by clicking on your account name and then choosing Lock.

- You can change your own account photo by displaying the Charms bar and then choosing the Settings icon. Click on the Change PC setting and choose Account picture. You can look for your own photos by clicking Browse, will let you browse the folders in your computer. Once you find the picture you want to use, click on Choose image to set it as your account picture. If you are running a laptop, you can also use the built-in webcam to take a picture of yourself for your account photo.

How to Customize the Start Screen Applications

You do not really need to put up with the pre-arranged apps on your Start screen. You can change how they look by rearranging them based on your own preference. You can move an app by clicking, holding and dragging the application to your preferred location. Let go of your mouse and the app tile will automatically move to the new place.

You may also think that the animation in the live tiles is very disturbing while you are working. Do not worry because you can simply turn the animation off so that you will only see a plain background. You can do this by right-clicking the application that you wish to change. A toolbar pop up from the bottom part of your computer screen. Simply choose Turn live tile off and the animation if you don't want real-time notifications.

How to Pin Applications to the Start Screen

By default, you won't be able to see all of the installed applications on the Start screen. However, you can easily "pin" your favorite apps on the Start screen so you can access them easily. You can do this by clicking the arrow found in the bottom-left corner of your Start screen. You will then see the list of all the applications that you have installed. Look for the app you want to pin and the right-click it. You will see Pin to Start at the lowest part of the screen. Click on it to pin your app.

To unpin or remove an application from the Start screen, right-click the app icon you want to remove and then choose "Unpin from Start".

How to Create Application Groups

There are more ways to bring organization to your apps. One way is to create an app group wherein you can similar apps together. You can give a specific name for each app group for easier retrieval. You can create a new application group by clicking, holding and dragging an application to the right side until you see it on an empty space of the Start screen. Let go of your mouse to let the app be inside its own application group. You will be able to see a distinct space between the new app group that you have just created and the other app groups. You can then drag other apps into the new group.

You can name your new application group by right clicking any of the apps on the Start screen and then clicking Name group at the top of the application group. When choosing a group name, opt for shorter, but more descriptive names. After you have keyed in your group name, press the Enter key.

Chapter 4: How to Manage Your Files and Folders

The File Explorer found in the Desktop view is very handy in managing files and folders in your computer. If you are familiar with older Windows version, File Explorer is actually the same as Windows Explorer. You will usually use the File Explorer for opening, accessing and rearranging folders and files in the Desktop view. You can launch the File Explorer by clicking the folder icon found on the taskbar.

The View tab in the File Explorer enables you to alter how the files appear inside the folders. For instance, you may choose to the List view when viewing documents and the Large Icons view when looking at photos. You can change the content view by selecting the View tab and then choosing your preferred view from the Layout group.

For certain folders, you can also sort your files in different ways – by name, size, file type, date modified, date created, among others. You can sort your files by selecting the View tab, clicking on the Sort by button and then choosing your preferred view from the drop-down list.

How to Search Using the File Explorer

Aside from using the Charms bar to look for files, you can also use the Search bar in the File Explorer. Actually, the File Explorer provides search options that are more advanced than those offered by the Charms bar. This is very useful when you are finding it quite hard to look for a particular document.

Every time you key in a word into the search bar, you will see that the Search Tools tab automatically opens on the Ribbon. You can find the advanced search options on the Search Tools tab. You can use them to filter your search by size, file type or date modified. You can also see the latest searches that you have made.

How to Work with Libraries

Windows 8 has 4 main libraries: Documents, Music, Pictures and Videos. Whenever you need a specific file, you can search for them through the Libraries or groups of content that you can readily access via the File Explorer.

The folders and files that you create are not actually stored in the Libraries themselves. The libraries are just there to help you better organize your stuff. You can place your own folders inside the libraries without the need to change their actual location in your computer. For instance, you can place a folder your recent photos in the Pictures library and still keep the folder on your Desktop for ready access.

Libraries are particularly vital in Windows 8 since a lot of the applications on the Start screen such as Photos, Music and Vides use the libraries in looking for and displaying their content. For instance, all of the photos in your Pictures library are also in your Photos app.

You need to note that the applications on your Start screen are optimized for media so that it will be more trouble-free for you to watch videos, listen to music and view your pictures. The File Explorer is an essential tool in organizing your current media files into libraries so that you can easily enjoy them right from your Start screen.

The My Music, My Documents folders and other certain folders are automatically included in their own applicable libraries. But you can add your own folders to any of the Libraries by first locating the Folder you want to add and then right-clicking on it. Choose the Include in library and then choose your preferred library. This technique allows your folder to be both in your library and in its original location.

Chapter 5: How to Get Started with the Desktop

The Start screen really is a cool new feature of Windows 8. But if you will be doing more than surfing the internet, watching videos and listening to music, you need to familiarize yourself with the different features in the Desktop view.

How to Work with Files

The details of the File Explorer were already discussed in the previous chapter. In this chapter, you will learn how to open and delete files, navigate through the various folders, and more.

After you have opened the File Explorer and you instantly see the document that you wish to open, you can simply double-click on it to open it. But if you still need to go through the different folders, the Navigation pane is very useful in choosing a different folder or location.

How to Delete Files

You can delete a file by clicking, holding and dragging the file directly to the Recycle Bin icon found on the Desktop. An easier way is choosing the file that you want to delete and then pressing the Delete key. Do not worry if you have unintentionally deleted a file. You can access the Recycle Bin to locate the deleted file and restore it to its original folder. You can do this by right-clicking the file that you want to restore and then choosing Restore.

But if you are certain that all files in the Recycle Bin can be permanently deleted, you can clear it by right-clicking the Recycle Bin icon and then choosing Empty Recycle bin.

How to Open an Application on the Desktop

You can do this by either clicking the application icon found on the taskbar or double-clicking the application shortcut found on the Desktop.

How to Pin Applications to the Taskbar

By default, only selected application icons will be included on your taskbar. But you can pin your most used application on the taskbar so you can readily access them. You can do this by right-clicking anyplace on the Start screen. You will then see a menu at the bottom of your screen. Choose the All apps button to show the list of all your installed applications. Look for the application you want to pin and the right-click it and then choose Pin to taskbar. You need to note, though, that you cannot pin all applications to your taskbar. There are certain applications that are designed to be launched from the Start screen only like Calendar and Messaging. Thus, you can only pin them to the Start screen.

How to Use Desktop Effects

Multi-tasking and working with several windows have become easier with Windows 8 because of the various Desktop effects now available to you.

- You can use the Snap effect to quickly resize open windows. This is particularly useful when you are working with several windows simultaneously. You can use the Snap effect by clicking, holding and dragging a window to the right or the left until you see the cursor reach the edge of your screen. Release your mouse to snap the window into place. You can easily unsnap a window by clicking, dragging it down and then releasing your mouse.

- Use the Peek effect for viewing the open windows from your taskbar. You can do this by hovering your mouse over any app icon on the taskbar that you want to view. You will then see a thumbnail preview of all open windows. You can view the full-sized window of the application by hovering the mouse over the app in the thumbnail preview.

- Use the Shake feature for selecting a single window from a clutter of open windows and then minimizing the rest. You can do this by locating and selecting the window that you want to concentrate on. You can then gently shake the window back and forth to minimize the other open windows. When you shake the window once more, all of the windows that you minimized will get maximized again.

- The Flip feature is useful in scrolling across a preview of all your open windows. You can also view any of the open applications on your Start screen using the Flip preview. The first three features – Snap, Shake and Peek – are for use only on the Desktop view. The Flip feature, on the other hand, can be used similarly in both the Desktop view and the Start screen. You can access the Flip preview by pressing and holding the Alt key and then pressing the Tab key. While you are still pressing the Alt key, press the Tab key to continue scrolling through your open windows. When you have spotted the application or the window that you want to view, stop pressing the Alt and Tab keys to display the app or window.

Conclusion

Thank you again for purchasing this book!

I hope this book was able to help you to use the new features of Windows 8.

The next step is to start personalizing your own Windows 8 so you can get the most out of it.

Finally, if you enjoyed this book, please take the time to share your thoughts and post a review on Amazon. We do our best to reach out to readers and provide the best value we can. Your positive review will help us achieve that. It'd be greatly appreciated!

Thank you and good luck!

Check Out My Other Books

Below you'll find some of my other popular books that are popular on Amazon and Kindle as well. Simply click on the links below to check them out. Alternatively, you can visit my author page on Amazon to see other work done by me.

C ++ Programming Success in a Day

Android Programming in a Day

PHP Programming Professional Made Easy

C Programming Success in a Day

CSS Programming Professional Made Easy

C Programming Professional Made Easy

JavaScript Programming Made Easy

HTML Professional Programming Made Easy

the rest of Python Programming in a Day

Programming Box Set #84: Facebook Social Power & Windows 8 Tips for Beginners

If the links do not work, for whatever reason, you can simply search for these titles on the Amazon website to find them.

www.ingramcontent.com/pod-product-compliance
Lightning Source LLC
Chambersburg PA
CBHW060931050326
40689CB00013B/3043
* 9 7 8 1 5 1 8 6 4 4 7 8 8 *